FREED

You can f   ___.

BIBLE STUDIES TO IMPACT THE LIVES OF ORDINARY PEOPLE

Written for The Word Worldwide
'Geared for Growth' series
by John Priddle

Preface

Welcome to this Word Worldwide 'Geared for Growth' Bible Study. It will encourage, challenge and enrich you as you follow it through. Its format makes it very suitable for group Bible study.

This study is made up of an Introduction and ten Bible studies on the theme of Freedom. Easy-to-read Bible passages indicated for each day are followed by questions to help stimulate a greater understanding of the Bible and encourage positive sharing.

It is strongly recommended that when used in groups, group members should first read the set daily Bible passages at home and answer the questions (writing the answers down will help in learning). During the group meeting these Bible passages should then be reread and answers to the questions shared. The appropriate page of Notes should be read at the end of the study period together.

An Answer Guide is included at the end of this booklet.

Contact your nearest address on page 40 if you would like help to set up and run a Bible study group. A *Guidelines for Group Leaders* leaflet is also available from the same address.

'Exposing as many people as possible to the truths of God's Word, using Geared for Growth Bible Studies as a tool for evangelism, spiritual growth and the imparting of missionary vision.'

National Library of Australia Card Number and ISBN 0 908067 02 X
© WEC International

Look up a dictionary and discuss the meaning given for 'freedom' or 'liberty'.

Any kind of life can thrive unrestrained when it is placed in its natural environment. Why do oranges grow well in Spain? Because the soil and climate provide the right warmth, moisture and nourishment for them.

Why are birds free in the air, and fish in water? Because they are in their natural elements. A fish out of water is in a desperate situation!

Human beings are only free to really live when they are in their proper element. The Bible tells us that mankind has lost the inner principle of life. Through disobedience we have forfeited our true environment – a life lived in unbroken fellowship with God. Look up and discuss these references – Genesis 3:3-11; Isaiah 59:2.

In order to be free from these limitations, provision has been made to bring us back into liberty. Look up and discuss Galatians 5:1.

We shall see in these studies how spiritual liberty is only possible to those who have life in Christ. When we receive new life in Him a threefold emancipation takes place.

1. The MIND is liberated through TRUTH.
   Contrast Ephesians 4:18 with John 8:32.
   All the human race fell into bondage when Adam accepted Satan's lie (Genesis 3:3 & 4). The only way back to freedom is through God's truth.
   We accept His Word with our MINDS, but life comes when we receive the ONE who is TRUTH.

2. The CONSCIENCE is liberated through PEACE.
   Read and discuss Hebrews 9:14; Hebrews 10:22; Titus 1:15.
   Guilt robs us of freedom and we stand condemned before God. But once our conscience is purged through the blood of the cross we are released into PEACE and find freedom from sin's condemnation.

3. The WILL is liberated through LOVE.
   It's always easy to do the things we LIKE doing. The more we like a thing (and liking, whether it's for ice-cream or sex can become uncontrolled desire!) the more we indulge. Instead of our wills controlling our lives, our feelings motivate our wills. We give in to what we love.

Scripture clearly teaches that we are in bondage to whatever controls our wills. Read and discuss Romans 6:16-18.
We shall discover that only when we are motivated by the love of right things are our wills freed from selfish and wrong directives. Paul says in 2 Corinthians 5:14: 'For Christ's love compels us'. So our wills must be liberated by divine love (Romans 5:5; John 17:26; Romans 13:10 and 1 John 4:16).

Real delight and freedom come from surrendering the will completely to Christ so that He is on the throne of our affections.

Whatever holds you captive and keeps you from enjoying a life of liberty in the Lord Jesus, can be swept away as you apply yourself earnestly to these studies. You will see that freedom is a paradox and you will pray, 'Make me a captive Lord, and then I shall be free', and learn to say:

> 'I'm free at last!
> Self had me tortured, twisted, tied in knots.
> Dejected in darkness
> But now I am free
> Now He has conquered
> And broken my fetters,

ABRAHAM – FREEDOM THROUGH OBEDIENCE

DAY 1   *Genesis 11:31-32.*

a) How many people left Ur of the Chaldeans to go to Canaan?
b) What happened when they got to Haran?

DAY 2   *Genesis 12:1; Acts 7:2-4; Hebrews 11:8.*

a) Where was Abraham when God first spoke to him?
b) Where did God tell him to go?

DAY 3   *Genesis 12:1-3; Isaiah 41:8-10.*

What did God promise him if he obeyed?

DAY 4   *Genesis 12:4-5.*

a) Why did Abraham leave Haran?
b) Who went with him?
c) How old was he went he set out?

DAY 5   *Genesis 12:6-7.*

a) How far had Abraham travelled when God spoke to him again (some Bibles may have a map section)?
b) What land did God promise to Abraham?
c) What feature of this land is noted?

DAY 6   *Genesis 12:7-8.*

a) What did Abraham do at Shechem, and then near Bethel?
b) Why do you think he did this?

DAY 7   *Genesis 26:2-5.*

a) God renewed the covenant relationship with Isaac, Abraham's son. How had Abraham merited this relationship?
b) Genesis 3:17. How did Adam lose the freedom of Eden?

Our topic is FREEDOM. In this first study we are considering Abraham, whom God called to enjoy the freedom of a covenant relationship with Himself.

1. Abraham's freedom was initiated by God
'The LORD had said ... Leave your country ... and go' (Genesis 12:1).
'You are the LORD God, who chose' (Nehemiah 9:7).
'Abraham my friend, I took you from the ends of the earth' (Isaiah 41:8-9).

2. Freedom from tradition
'Leave your country, your people ...'
When we compare several passages of Scripture, (Genesis 15:7; Acts 7:2; Nehemiah 9:7) we find that God appeared to Abraham while he was living in Ur of the Chaldeans.

Archaeologists, notably Sir Charles Woolley in 1929, have made startling discoveries about the civilization which existed in Ur of the Chaldeans in the days of Abraham. The dwellings of the wealthy were large two-storeyed villas with 13 or 14 rooms, and Ur apparently was a prosperous, busy capital city.
A reconstruction of the ziggurat (temple) shows it to be a huge square edifice, 75 feet high, with sides 120 feet long. Above a black foundation rose the red and blue of the upper stages, lined with trees, and capped by a golden roofed Holy Place dedicated to the moon-god, Nannar.

3. Freedom to worship God
We can appreciate the wisdom of God in freeing Abraham from idol-worshipping traditions.

Joshua 24:2 tells us that 'Terah, the Father of Abraham ... worshipped other gods.'

The fact that Joshua still had to tell his contemporaries to, 'Throw away the gods your forefathers worshipped beyond the River and in Egypt' (Joshua 24:14), shows that some of Abraham's party brought their idols with them. Abraham, however, like some of Paul's converts centuries later, 'turned to God from idols, to serve the living and true God' (1 Thessalonians 1:9).

As soon as Abraham reached Canaan, he 'built an altar there to the LORD' (Genesis 12:7). At the next stop he also worshipped (Genesis 12:8) and on returning from Egypt he again 'called on the name of the LORD' (Genesis 13:4).

4. Freedom through obedience
How was Abraham's freedom obtained? Simply and directly we are told that Abraham's freedom was the outcome of his obedience to God's word: 'So Abraham left, as the

LORD had told him' (Genesis 12:4); 'because Abraham obeyed me' (Genesis 26:5). 'By faith Abraham, when called to go ... obeyed and went' (Hebrews 11:8).

In Ezekiel's day when the Israelites were in captivity, they accused God of being unfair. They said: 'Abraham was only one man, yet he possessed the land (symbolical of freedom). But we are many; surely the land has been given to us as our possession' (Ezekiel 33:24)

God told Ezekiel why the people did not enjoy the freedom that Abraham had. He said: 'With their mouths they express devotion, but their hearts are greedy for unjust gain' (Ezekiel 33:31).

5. By contrast – bondage through disobedience

One might say that Adam was 'born free', however, this was within the context of man's complete dependence on his Creator. (Genesis 2:7-9)

The freedom of Eden had but one limitation: 'You are free to eat from any tree in the garden; but ...' (Genesis 2:16-17).

Would Adam obey or disobey?

His freedom depended on the choice he made.

The result of his disobedience was twofold:

(1) He lost his own freedom (Genesis 3:17,19)

(2) 'through the disobedience of the one man the many were made sinners' (Romans 5:19).

To say 'no' to God is to forfeit the freedom He offers.

To say 'yes' brings the glorious promise given to Abraham: 'I will bless you' (Genesis 12:2).

'So do not fear, for I am with you,
do not be dismayed, for I am your God.
I will strengthen you and help you;
I will uphold you with my righteous right hand'
(Isaiah 41:10).

FREEDOM FROM BONDAGE

DAY 1 *Exodus 1*
a) Why were the Israelites desperate for God to intervene in the life of their nation?
b) Exodus 2:11-15. Who tried to help them and initially failed?

DAY 2 *Exodus 12:1-6.*
a) What did God tell the people of Israel to do?
b) What was to be special about the animal chosen? In what way would this prefigure the life of the Lord Jesus (Isaiah 53:9; John 8:46)?

DAY 3 *Exodus 12:7-13.*
a) What was the only protection the Israelites would have on the night of the slaughter?
b) How is Jesus described in 1 Corinthians 5:7?
c) Why was it not possible for Christ's life alone to free us from sin (1 Peter 1:18-19)?

DAY 4 *Exodus 12:21-23.*
a) God's instructions must have seemed very strange. Would you have obeyed if you had been there?
b) Hebrews 11:28. Why was the 'Passover' so called?

DAY 5 *Exodus 12:24-28.*
a) Why do you think the people were told to keep on remembering this Passover night?
b) 1 Corinthians 11:23-26. What do believers specially remember in the Lord's Supper (Communion service)?

DAY 6 *Exodus 12:29-33.*
a) How are the Egyptians a picture of those who do not trust in the redeeming work of Christ (Hebrews 9:22)?
b) How do these verses prove the truth of Psalm 76:10?

DAY 6 *Exodus 12:34-42.*
a) What does this passage tell us the people of Israel did?
b) Freedom from bondage results in a going forward. Can you apply this to our freedom in Christ (1 Peter 2:16)?

The scene is set in the land of Egypt. For 400 years the people of Israel have been a nation of slaves, in bondage. Now God's appointed time has come, and God's people are to be set free. The deliverance comes, not from Moses, who said: 'O Lord, please send someone else to do it' (Exodus 4:13), nor from Pharaoh, who said: 'I will not let Israel go' (Exodus 5:2), nor from the people themselves, who said to Moses: 'Leave us alone; let us serve the Egyptians' (Exodus 14:12).

The deliverance comes from God: 'The LORD brought the Israelites out of Egypt' (Exodus 12:51). Before it happened He said to Moses: 'I will use my mighty power and perform great miracles to deliver them from slavery, and make them free ... And they shall know that I am Jehovah their God who has rescued them' (Exodus 6:6-7, LB). The whole story is a mighty picture of a spiritual truth.

FREEDOM IS COSTLY
The lamb had to be perfect without blemish. It was to be a substitute, killed so that the eldest son would live. Josephus the historian records that Moses killed the Passover lamb between the ninth and the eleventh hour (see Matthew 27:45-50).

FREEDOM IS ONLY OBTAINED GOD'S WAY
There had to be exact obedience to God's commands. There was nothing else to trust for protection, except the blood on the door-posts. There was no other way for people to escape the judgment of God: 'Look, the Lamb of God, who takes away the sin of the world' (John 1:29).

FREEDOM IS NOT TO BE TAKEN FOR GRANTED
The people of Israel were not to forget what God had done. They were to teach their children about God's great redemption. They were to retain a spirit of gratitude to God.

* * * *

Many times in the Bible God uses this deliverance of His people as an example of His might and power: 'I am the LORD your God, who brought you up out of Egypt' (Psalm 81:10). The Psalmists, prophets and leaders also delighted to extol the Lord in this way: 'Nothing is too hard for you ... You brought your people Israel out of Egypt ... by a mighty hand and an outstretched arm' (Jeremiah 32:17,21). Sometimes the people claimed God's interest in them by reference to this incident: 'Now, O Lord our God, who brought your people out of Egypt with a mighty hand ... we do not make requests of you because we are righteous, but because of your great mercy' (Daniel 9:15-18).

In the New Testament, God's mighty act of deliverance is still remembered: 'He (God) led them out of Egypt and did wonders and miraculous signs in Egypt' (Acts 7:36). The RESULT of Israel's freedom was the birth of a new nation, God's own people, free to do God's will and accomplish His purposes. So it is with the Christian: 'Therefore, if anyone is in Christ, he is a new creation'; he is free to serve God.

FREEDOM THROUGH FAITH

DAY 1 *Joshua 2:1-7.*

a) Did Rahab know the spies were coming to Jericho?

b) Was she afraid to receive them?

c) What do you think was the difference between Rahab's reply about the men (vv. 4-5) and Abraham's reply to Isaac (Genesis 22:7-8)?

DAY 2 *Joshua 2:8-11.*

a) What three events had revealed God's wonder-working to the Canaanites?

b) How had Rahab and her people reacted to these events? What did Rahab know would happen?

DAY 3 *Joshua 2:11.*

a) Compare verse 11b with Matthew 16:17. What similarity is there between them?

b) Would you say that a revelation of God was beginning to set Rahab free?

c) What did Jesus say sets people free (John 8:32)? (Would you like to share any truth about God that has particularly impressed you?)

DAY 4 *Joshua 2:12-14.*

a) What drove Rahab to seek to make a pact with the spies?

b) Genesis 2:17; Matthew 10:28. What death is more serious than physical death? From which death could the spies only save her?

d) Did the spies have any doubt that Israel would overthrow Jericho?

DAY 5 *Joshua 2:15-18.*

a) What was Rahab to do to ensure her own safety and that of her family?

b) Exodus 12:7,13. Do you see a similarity here? How are we delivered from divine judgment today (John 3:18,36; Acts 16:30-31)?

DAY 6 *Joshua 2:18-24.*

a) How did Rahab ensure she would be safe when Jericho would fall.

b) When is it time for us to act to be assured of eternal salvation (2 Corinthians 6:2)? Why is this (Proverbs 27:1)?

c) What word of faith did the spies take back to Joshua? Compare this with Numbers 13:30-31.

DAY 7 *Joshua 6:24-25; Hebrews 11:31.*

a) Did God reward Rahab's obedience of faith?

b) Matthew 1:5. What great plan had God in mind for Rahab the prostitute?

c) Joshua 24:15. Is this the motto in your household?

Joshua, sent out as one of the original spies (Numbers 13) now sends out two more spies. They are to find out how best to cross the flooded River Jordan and tackle the Canaanites on its western bank. Naturally their mission was top secret. Rahab would therefore have known nothing of their coming. Her home was on the wall overlooking the city and would be a likely vantage point for the spying out of the land. Rahab recognised the spies to be Israelites and had no compunction either about hiding them or lying to protect them. Her action gives no room for Christians to lie or deceive, but she, as a heathen woman, had no hesitation about doing either.

This woman lost no time in declaring her belief that Israel's God was great. She knew of the deliverance at the Red Sea (Exodus 14:21-25) and the defeat of Sihon and Og (Deuteronomy 2:32-34 and 3:1-2). This recognition of God ultimately led to salvation for her and her household. But the incidents which drew Rahab to faith, paralysed her people with fear. We see the truth about the one true God dawning on Rahab's pagan heart just as clearly as the revelation came to Peter that Christ was the Son of God (Matthew 16:17).

Knowing that her nation would eventually be overcome by Israel, Rahab feared both for her own life and that of her family. This is why she sought to make a pact with the spies. The God who was drawing her to Himself would preserve her for His purposes we know, but Rahab, human-like, was at that stage trying to save her own skin. The spies, urging her to secrecy about their mission, made a plan for her safety, at the same time evidencing their own faith in God (v.14).

The red cord, symbol of salvation, reminds us of the Passover story. Here the blood on the door-posts of the obedient Israelites spared them God's judgment (Exodus 12:13). The picture points to Calvary and Christ's redeeming blood shed for us (Ephesians 1:7; Hebrews 9:13-14; Mark 14:22,25; Romans 3:25; 5:9; 1 Corinthians 11:25). Later, in Joshua 6:25 we see that the bargain was kept and Rahab and her household were saved and engrafted into the nation of Israel. The Bible narrative, picking up the genealogy of Christ in Matthew 1, shows that Jesus came via Mary (v.16) and David (v.6) and the heathen woman Rahab (v.5) who was liberated by her faith in God.

Throughout the New Testament we see examples of faith that brings deliverance and find constant encouragement to believe in Him: Matthew 9:22; 15:22-28; 21:21-22; Mark 11:22; Luke 7:50; 22:32; Romans 1:17; 1 John 5:4.

> 'My faith looks up to Thee.
> Thou Lamb of Calvary,
> Saviour Divine!
> Now hear me while I pray,
> Take all my guilt away,
> O may I from this day
> Be wholly Thine.'

SET FREE TO SERVE

DAY 1   *Exodus 3:1-10.*

a) What had the Israelites become in Egypt?
b) What was God going to do for them?
c) How did He purpose to do this (v.10)?

DAY 2   *Acts 26:17-18; Ephesians 2:1-3.*

a) What type of slavery is referred to here? Who are the slaves and would you say these slaves are happy people?
b) Why can we do nothing to free ourselves (Ephesians 2:8)?

DAY 3   *Romans 5:1-12.*

a) Are we sinners just because we do wrong things (v.12)?
b) What hope does the person who is a slave to sin have (vv.6,8)?
c) How do we become free from sin (vv.1-2)?

DAY 4   *Romans 6:15-18.*

a) What does Paul say of both the person who sins and the one who lives righteously?
b) Why is Paul thankful.
c) Could Paul be speaking of you in verse 18?

DAY 5   *Romans 6:19-23.*

a) Would you say that the Christian is still a slave?
b) What is the basis of this new relationship (2 Corinthians 5:14-15)?
c) What does our new Master give us?
d) What are Christians urged to do in verse 19b and Romans 12:1-2?

DAY 6   *Exodus 21:1-6.*

a) What choice did Hebrew servants have after 6 years?
b) Why did some refuse to go free? What happened to them?
c) How is a Christian like the servant to refused to go free?

DAY 7   *1 Thessalonians 1.*

a) How did Paul describe the dramatic change that had taken place in the lives of these Thessalonians (v.9)?
b) As servants of God what were they now doing?

We have seen in a previous study how God called Abraham to be father of His chosen people and purposed to bless them and make them great. Even in Egypt God had so blessed and prospered His people that the Egyptians became jealous and afraid of their wealth and power. They determined to cripple Israel by subjecting them to arduous toil and making them poverty-stricken slaves. Now Israel comes to God in her affliction, longing to be delivered, and God calls Moses to plead her cause before Pharaoh and lead her out of Egypt (Exodus 2:23-25; 3:10).

The whole picture of Israel's bondage brings forcibly to us the plight of all mankind. Held in the bondage of sin, unable to do anything to break free (Ephesians 2:1-6: can a dead person do anything?), God planned deliverance through Christ (Romans 3:25).

Later, when Israel had been brought out from Egypt, we find God setting down regulations for their spiritual and national life. Among directions given were those on the handling of their own servants or slaves. Of particular interest to us is the fact that every seven years a slave was offered his freedom. However, if he loved his master and wished to remain in his service he became a bond slave for life (Exodus 21:5) and the mark of his chosen servitude was put upon him (Exodus 21:6).

Again, this is the picture of the individual, who, faced up with the issue of his slavery to sin, is offered freedom through the Lord Jesus Christ. Forsaking sin, accepting deliverance from his bondage to Satan, in love and gratitude he yields himself a bondservant to Christ. The supreme example of this in Scriptures is Christ Himself. Though very God, He yielded Himself up to God and in so doing became a servant and was made in the likeness of man for man's redemption (Philippians 2:6-8) and carries even in His resurrected body the marks of His servitude (John 20:25,27). Paul also declared himself to be a bond slave of Christ (Romans 1:1) and bore the marks of His servitude with joy (Galatians 6:17).

Jeremiah 17:9 describes the heart of each human being and Scripture bears out the fact of our miserable state (Romans 3:10-18) and the result of such a life (Romans 6:23a). Romans 6 clearly sets out the key to deliverance. Here Paul shows us that we can only be set free through Christ (John 8:36) and that, being set free from the bondage of sin we enter into a new living, loving relationship, freely choosing to be servants of Christ and His righteousness (Romans 6:18).

From studying these Scriptures we can only be convinced that true freedom really results from servitude to the right master. Adam's deed of self-assertion (Genesis 3:6) brought all men into self-will, slavery to sin and the devil (Romans 5:12,14) and spiritual death (Romans 5:15). But Christ's act of self-sacrifice bestows free and unmerited favour upon the one who trusts in Him (Romans 5:16) and ushers in for each believer 'a reign of life' (Romans 5:17).

The glorious truth is that cowering, cringing slaves of sin and death can become, through grace, slaves of God, reigning with Christ (Ephesians 2:6) and joint heirs in His inheritance (Romans 8:17).

Pray that God, by His Spirit will reveal this truth to you in fullest measure, setting you free entirely from the bondage which Satan has had over you. Christ says the same to us today as He said to His disciples of old in Mark 8:34-36. And having done this, yield yourself to His Lordship as Paul pleads in Romans 12:1-2.

> 'Make me a captive, Lord, and then I shall be free.
> Force me to render up my sword and I shall conqueror be.
> I sink in life's alarms when by myself I stand,
> Imprison me within thine arms and strong shall be my hand.'

FREEDOM DESPITE CIRCUMSTANCES

DAY 1   *Daniel 3:1-7.*

a) Why had so many people come together in the plain of Dura?

b) What would motivate the people to fall down and worship the golden image?

DAY 2   *Daniel 2:48-48; 3:8-12.*

a) Why do you think these Chaldeans (astrologers) told the king about the three Jews?

b) How did Jesus respond to those who were seeking to harm him (Isaiah 53:7; 1 Peter 2:21-23)?

DAY 3   *Daniel 3:13-15.*

a) Picture the scene described in these verses. What doubt did the king try instil into the minds of Shadrach, Meshach and Abednego?

b) Compare this with the story in Matthew 14:25-32. What happened when Peter began to doubt the Lord's power?

DAY 4   *Daniel 3:16-18.*

a) What were these three men determined not to do? What example have they set for us?

b) How would you explain the fearlessness of Peter and John in Acts 4:13-20?

DAY 5   *Daniel 3:19-23.*

a) Notice that God did not work a miracle to make the king change his mind. What happened?

b) What does God's Word tell us to do in times of trial (1 Peter 4:12-19)?

DAY 6   *Daniel 3:24-27.*

a) What was it that amazed and terrified King Nebuchadnezzar?

b) Read Isaiah 43:1-5 through three times. To whom do these promises apply?

DAY 7   *Daniel 3:28-30.*

a) What three things did the king acknowledge these men had done?

b) What affect did their unflinching loyalty to God have?

'You are commanded that you shall ... or else ...!' Try to imagine yourself in such a situation. Freedom? Far from it!

What would you have done? Kept the peace, and bowed down? What harm would there be in it, if you didn't tell anyone you were worshipping God in private?

Think of some countries today. If a man is known to be a Christian, he loses his job, his children 'fail' their examinations, they are indoctrinated against their parents' beliefs, and the family is ostracised. At the smallest excuse, he will be put in prison and tortured. His wife will be refused work, there will be no money coming in.

If that were your situation, would you continue to worship God and teach your children to love Him? If, instead, you kept on the right side of the authorities, where would this lead? How would your children grow up? Would this bring you freedom?

Shadrach, Meshach and Abednego had to make the decision. Notice how their very words and manner revealed that they were free men. In effect they said: 'God has given us freedom and peace of mind. You cannot take it away. The Lord will either deliver us, or take us to be with Him; either way, we have nothing to lose'.

During severe persecution under Communism in Russia someone wrote: 'We are more powerful than the Communists. Greater courage and power is needed to face a whipping with a smile, than to do the whipping! Let them hate us, but we will love them.' Are not these the words of a person who is truly free?

> 'Stone walls do not a prison make,
> Nor iron bars a cage;
> Minds innocent and quiet take
> That for a hermitage;
> If I have freedom in my love
> And in my soul am free,
> Angels alone, that soar above,
> Enjoy such liberty.'
> (Richard Lovelace, 17th Century)

Is this inner freedom, given by God, less of a miracle than what happened when Shadrach, Meshach and Abednego were thrown into the furnace?

Miracles are characterised by three things: wonder, power and significance.

The significance of this miracle was to show the sovereignty of the true God over the nation which had taken Israel captive. It also showed His power, in keeping His servants free from even the smell of smoke! This was a physical demonstration, to show the way in which the Lord can keep us free from evil, free from fear and free from the power of death, even in the most adverse circumstances.

JESUS, THE LIBERATOR

DAY 1   *Luke 4:14-15.*
a) 'Jesus returned to Galilee.' Previous to this, what two important events had taken place in Jesus' life (Luke 3:21-22; 4:1-2) ?
b) What does Luke record about Jesus in verse 15?

DAY 2   *Luke 4:16-21.*
a) What did Jesus deliberately do when given the Isaiah scroll to read from?
b) Isaiah 61:1-2. Where did Jesus stop His reading from Isaiah? What then did He omit to read? Why do you think He did this (John 12:47)?
c) What was his first comment on the passage He had just read?

DAY 3   *Luke 4:18-19; John 8:31-36.Luke 4:20.*
a) What needy categories of people are listed here? What would Jesus do for each of them?
b) Under whose authority was Jesus acting?

DAY 4   *John 8:31-38.*
a) What kind of slavery is mentioned here?
b) How is release obtained from this kind of slavery?

DAY 5   *2 Corinthians 4:4; Ephesians 4:18.*
a) What kind of blindness is described here? Why is a serious blindness?
b) Who did Jesus claim to be (John 8:12)?

DAY 6   *Luke 4:22.*
a) Why were the people amazed?
b) What limited view had they of Jesus (Matthew 13:53-58)?

DAY 7   *Luke 4:23-30.*
a) Why do you think the widow in Zarephath and Naaman were specifically mentioned?
b) Jesus wanted to liberate these people from their spiritual need. What did the people try to do to Him instead?
c) Do you think people are irritated by Jesus today.

In this study we take a look at Jesus the Liberator. He claimed that He had come 'to set the captives free'. What did He mean? Who were the captives? From what were they to be set free? In order to set another free, one must be free oneself. Was Jesus a truly free man in every way? Who was Jesus?

His Stupendous Claims

We cannot logically agree with those who say that Jesus was just a 'good man'. He made claims about Himself that would be pretentious for any human being to make. Either He was what He claimed to be, or He was a liar and a deceiver. He could not have been simply a 'good man'.

He said: 'I came from God' (John 8:42); 'I and the Father are one' (John 10:30); 'No-one comes to the Father, except through me' (John 14:6).

His enemies used as their trump card the fact that He claimed to be the Son of God (John 19:7, also John 6:35-40). In Luke 4:18,21 He claimed to be the Messiah, the Anointed One, who had come to set the captives free. He also said: 'If you hold to my teaching ... Then you will know the truth, and the truth will set you free' (John 8:31-33); 'So if the Son sets you free, you will be free indeed' (John 8:36).

His Purpose in Coming to Earth

Before Jesus' birth the angel said to Joseph: 'he will save his people from their sins' (Matthew 1:21). He Himself said that He had come, to bind Satan and release his captives (Matthew 12:29; Luke 11:17-22).

John records: 'The reason the Son of God appeared was to destroy the devil's work' (1 John 3:8). Hebrews 2:14 adds that He could only do this through His death. We know from Study 2 that it was only when the Passover Lamb was killed, that its blood could save. How triumphant was that cry from the Cross when Jesus knew that He had accomplished what He had come to earth to do ... 'It is finished.' The Apostle Paul reminds us often that Christ has set us free (Galatians 5:1; Romans 8:2, 2 Corinthians 3:17).

The Freedom He Enjoyed

A person who is in bondage himself cannot set others free. Jesus was the one completely free man.

He was free from: any sense of inferiority (John 7:15-17), Jewish prejudice (John 10:16), the rigidity of the law (Matthew 5:38-39), fear (John 19:8-12), arrogance or pride (John 13:12-16), impulsiveness (John 18:10-11), self-centredness (Luke 22:42), sin (1 Peter 2:22) ... and so we could go on. He was even free to lay down His life, and free to take it again (John 10:17-18).

What is your most enslaving habit? What besetting sin do you long to be tree from? Jesus, who was free of this Himself, longs to set you free. Will you let Him?

FREEDOM FROM FEAR

DAY 1   *Matthew 10:28.*
a) What two kinds of death are spoken of here?
b) Which are we told to fear?
c) Which kind is referred to in John 8:51 and Genesis 3:3?

DAY 2   *Genesis 3:1-8; 3:23-24.*
a) What consequence of Adam and Eve's sin is highlighted here?
b) 1 John 3:14; John 5:24; 17:3. How is coming back into fellowship with
    God described?

DAY 3   *1 Corinthians 15:12-19,32; Matthew 25:31-32,46.*
a) What mistake do some people make about physical death.
b) How did Jesus show that physical death does not end everything?

DAY 4   *2 Corinthians 3:18; 4:16.*
a) What difference is highlighted between the physical and spiritual life of a
    Christian?
b) Isaiah 41:10; Hebrews 13:5; Romans 8:38-39. What is promised to those
    who belong to God?

DAY 5   *Hebrews 12:2; Romans 8:18; 2 Corinthians 12:9; 4:17-18; Hebrews 2:18.*
a) How was Jesus able to endure the cross?
b) How can He free us from fear in time of suffering?

DAY 6   *Hebrews 2:15; Romans 8:11; 1 Corinthians 15:55-57; Philippians 1:21-23.*
a) What kind of fear is mentioned in Hebrews 2:15?
b) How can a Christian have victory over this fear?

DAY 7   *Mark 4:35-40; Acts 27:13-25.*
a) Discuss the potential for fear in each of these situations.
b) How do they show that faith and trust in God in difficult situations can
    bring calm?

Have you ever noticed how often we read in the Bible 'Fear not', 'Don't be afraid'? It has been said that there are 365 'fear nots' in the Bible, one for every day in the year. It is always God, or God's servant, or God's messenger, who calms those who are fearful with an assurance that God has an answer to every problem. 'Do not be afraid, Abram, I am your shield' (Genesis 15:1). 'What is the matter, Hagar? Do not be afraid, God has heard the boy crying' (Genesis 21:17).

From Genesis to Revelation, the reassuring words of God Almighty ring out, speaking also to us today, culminating in the ultimate reason for assurance: 'Do not be afraid. I am the First and the Last. I am the Living One; I was dead, and behold I am alive for ever and ever! And I hold the keys of death and Hades' (Revelation 1:17, 18). Jesus Himself was free from fear, and He came to set men free from fear also. His work in us is to bring us from fear into faith (Mark 4:40).

We fear what we don't understand. We fear what lies ahead, cloaked in mystery. It is natural for man to fear the 'last enemy' (1 Corinthians 15:26) death.

Why has God put this fear of physical death in our hearts? Surely it is to teach us to fear **spiritual death**, a far more terrifying thing and to seek the relationship with God which is eternal life beginning here and now (John 3:36).

Jesus said 'I am the resurrection and the life. He who believes in me will live, even though he dies (physically); and whoever lives and believes in me will never die (spiritually)' (John 11:25-26). Do you believe this? Physical death is temporary separation from loved ones. Spiritual death is eternal separation from God.

The story is told of the English Reformation martyr, John Hooper, as he was being led to the stake. Well meaning friends pleaded with him to recant, saying, 'Life is sweet and death is bitter'. 'Oh, yes,' he replied, 'but eternal life is more sweet, and eternal death more bitter.'

When we see that eternal life is a close, personal relationship with Jesus, and that nothing, absolutely nothing can separate us from Him ever again (Romans 8:38-39), doesn't this take the fear out of physical death? Death makes no difference to the relationship between Christ and the believer. If we can say, 'For to me, to live is Christ' then we can honestly say also, 'to die is gain' (Philippians 1:21).

So it is **faith** and **trust** which are the antidotes to **fear**. If I have completely handed over the control of my life to Christ, if He is to me, 'my Shepherd', then I can confidently say, 'I will fear no evil, for you are with me' (Psalm 23:1,4).

'Do not be anxious about anything, but in everything, by prayer and petition, with thanksgiving, present your requests to God. And the peace of God, which transcends all understanding will guard your hearts and your minds in Christ Jesus' (Philippians 4:6-7).

FREEDOM FROM SELF AND SIN

DAY 1   *Romans 3:23; 5:12.*
a) What fact of sin is stressed here?
b) List some of the sins mentioned in Romans 1:22-32.

DAY 2   *Romans 5:12-19.*
a) How did sin enter the human race (v.12; Genesis 3:6-10)?
b) What effect has Adam's disobedience had on us (v.19)?
c) Can we assume that we are quite sinless till we do something wrong (Psalm 51:5; Ephesians 2:1-3)?

DAY 3   *Genesis 3:10-12; Isaiah 14:12-14; Luke 12:16-20.*
a) What little word in these three readings hits you about Adam, Satan and the rich man?
b) What does this word indicate about the real nature of sin (Genesis 3:5)?

DAY 4   *Romans 8:1-13.*
a) Who cannot please God (v.8)?
b) If we persist in living independently of God (as sin was defined yesterday) what must be our end (v.6)?
c) John 8:44; 1 John 3:10. If we act independently of God, to whom are we really giving allegiance?

DAY 5   *2 Corinthians 5:14b-15,21.*
a) What do these verses tell us about the Lord Jesus?
b) How is a Christian expected to live (v.15)?

DAY 6   *2 Corinthians 5:17-21.*
a) How is a Christian described in verse 17? (Is it describing you?)
b) What new form of service will a life centred around Christ become involved in?

DAY 7   Philippians 3:1,7-11.
a) Which evidently gave Paul the greatest joy: pleasing himself (Acts 26:9), or serving Christ?
b) Matthew 16:24-27. When we give up what 'we' want and follow Christ, what do we gain?

In Romans 5 and 6 we see clearly contrasted life in Adam and life in Christ. Adam in disobedience brought spiritual death (eternal separation from God) upon himself and all who descended from him (Romans 5:12). Christ in obedience fulfils God's plan of salvation (Philippians 2:8) and restores the believer to a right relationship with God.

Born of the flesh and sinful in Adam, God has provided for us to be 'born again' of the Spirit into Christ (1 Peter 1:23) and restored to His image (1 John 3:2), the image which He originally intended for us (Genesis 1:27). The great gap between these two can be bridged only by the Cross. The liberating work of Christ in this respect has been studied already. The chart on the following page will help us see more clearly the transforming work which takes place when by faith, forsaking our old relationship, we enter into the new relationship in Christ (Romans 6:11). The lists by no means exhaust what the Bible says of either state. Perhaps you would like to pursue the study with the use of a concordance and find out more about your inheritance in Christ. Read the references in various translations for further clarity.

Doesn't this study encourage us to be bond slaves of Christ and not of Satan?

> Buried with Christ, and raised with Him too:
> What is there left for me to do?
> Simply to cease from struggling and strife.
> Simply to walk in newness of life.
>
> Risen with Christ, my glorious Head.
> Holiness now the pathway I tread.
> Beautiful thought, while walking therein:
> He that is dead is freed from sin.
>
> Living with Christ, who dieth no more.
> Following Christ, who goeth before:
> I am from bondage utterly freed,
> Reckoning self as dead indeed.
>
> Living for Christ, my members I yield.
> Servants to God, for evermore sealed,
> Not under law, I'm now under grace.
> Sin is dethroned, and Christ takes its place.
>
> Growing in Christ; no more shall be named
> Things of which now I'm truly ashamed:
> Fruit unto holiness will I bear,
> Life evermore, the end I shall share.

ADAM

Created in the image of God (Genesis 1:27)
Alienated from God by self-choosing
(Genesis 3:6-8)
Dead to God (Genesis 3:3)

MANKIND IN ADAM

Ungodly (Romans 5:6)
Sinners (Romans 5:8)
Enemies of God (Romans 5:10)
Dead in sin (Romans 5:15)
Condemned (Romans 5:8)
Slaves of sin (Romans 6:20)
Carnal (Romans 7:14)
Sold under sin (Romans 7:14)
Without goodness (Romans 7:18)
Unable to do good (Romans 7:19)
Capable of evil (Romans 7:19)
Wretched (Romans 7:24)
Productive of: (Galatians 5:19-21)
Impure thoughts
Lust
Idolatry
Spiritism
Hatred
Fightings
Jealousy
Anger
Greed
Complaints
Criticism
Envy
Murder
Drunkenness, etc.
and at the end ...
DEATH (Romans 6:23)

CHRIST

God with us (Matthew 1:23)
Delivering us through self-giving
(Philippians 2:8)
Reigning in power (Ephesians 1:20-22)

BELIEVERS IN CHRIST

Walking in newness of life (Romans 6:4)
Partakers of the resurrection (Romans 6:5)
Freed from sin (Romans 6:7)
Freed from sin's dominion (Romans 6:13)
Alive with Him (Romans 6:8)
Dead to sin (Romans 6:11)
Alive from the dead (Romans 6:13)
Servants of God (Romans 6:18, 22)
Inheritors of eternal life (Romans 6:23)
Spiritually minded (Romans 8:6)
Partakers of life and peace (Romans 8:6)
Led by Spirit of God (Romans 8:14)
Adopted into God's family (Romans 8:15)
Children of God (Romans 8:16)
Heirs of God (Romans 8:17)
Joint Heirs with Christ (Romans 8:17)
Productive of fruits of the Spirit:
(Galatians 5:22-24)
Love
Joy
Peace
Patience
Kindness
Goodness
Faith
Humility
Self-control
and our end ...
ETERNAL LIFE (Romans 6:23)

FREEDOM FROM THE LAW

DAY 1   *Romans 7:7,13.*
a) What does the law do for us?
b) Galatians 3:24. How does the law lead us to Christ?

DAY 2   *Galatians 3:10-13.*
a) Why are we guilty in the eyes of the law (Romans 3:23)?
b) What does the law do to those who fail to keep it?

DAY 3   *Romans 7:5,7-12.*
a) How does sin take advantage of the law?
b) Is the law to blame for this?

DAY 4   *Galatians 3:15-16,21.*
a) What do these verses emphasise about the law?
b) Philippians 3:4-10. What did Paul regard as more important than trying to keep the law?

DAY 5   *Romans 7:1-4.*
a) What releases a woman to marry again?
b) Whose death is required to release us from the law?

DAY 6   *Romans 6:15; 7:4-6; Galatians 2:19; 5:13.*
a) Does freedom from the law mean that we can live as we please?
b) What does freedom from the law release us to do?

DAY 7   *Galatians 3:;1-5.*
a) Why was Paul upset with the Galatians?
b) What were they reminded they had gained through believing which could not have been achieved through trying to keep the law?

The word *law* used in the Bible means instruction given to men by God through selected people such as Moses, priests, prophets or other 'servants of the Lord'. After the nation of Israel had been brought out of Egypt, God gave, through Moses, very specific instructions governing both their religious and social life. The books which span Moses' lifetime are called the 'Books of the Law', but the Old Testament and sometimes the whole Bible, is spoken of as the 'Law of God'.

Quite specifically, in Exodus 20, the Ten Commandments are set forth as the law of God. From them we see that God expects perfection from His people. Later, in Leviticus 19, it states 'Be holy because I, the LORD your God, am holy'. In spite of God's injunction that they are to be holy, He obviously knows they won't be, because alongside the commandments He makes provision for their sins (Leviticus 4:2-3). So the nation of Israel was constantly reminded of the holiness of God, God's desire that they be holy, their own sinfulness and God's provision of a sacrifice for sin.

The Bible reiterates this message over and over again. In the New Testament God says: 'without holiness no-one will see the Lord' (Hebrews 12:14); 'for all have sinned and fall short of the glory of God' (Romans 3:23); 'If anybody does sin, we have one who speaks to the Father in our defence' (1 John 2:1).

What purpose does the law serve then if it shows God's holiness and we can't attain to that? The answer is given in Romans 7:7,15,16. Here it says that because the law shows what I should do, I am made conscious of the fact that I don't do it. Conversely, what I shouldn't do, I do.

A toddler will very happily pull dad's best blooms apart and say 'pretty'. When he is cautioned, maybe ultimately smacked, he may continue to destroy the flowers, but less happily for he sees the red warning light flashing and knows that the hand of the law will be after him again!

'So the law was put in charge to lead us to Christ' is the way Paul puts it (Galatians 3:24). In other words, the law teaches me where I fall short of God's standard. Ultimately we should all get to the place Paul reached in Romans 7:24, where we cry to God to show us the way. We know we haven't got what it takes to live up to God's holy standards.

Galatians 3:25 tells us that when *faith* has come we are no longer under the supervision of the law. How does faith free us from the law? Christ is the end of the law to everyone who believes (Romans 10:4). Christ fully satisfies God's holy standards. Now I, by believing that I can accept Christ's death as my death and Christ's rising from the dead as my rising to new life in Him (Romans 6) am released from the law by faith. The RSV reads that we are 'discharged from the law, dead to that which held us captive' (Romans 7:4).

'Free from the law, oh, happy condition! Jesus has bled, and there is remission. Cursed by the law, and bruised by the Fall, Grace has redeemed us once for all.'

GLORIOUS FREEDOM

DAY 1 *Romans 8:1-4.*
a) Who are free from condemnation (v.1)?
b) What are we set free from?
c) What did God do to set us free?

DAY 2 *Romans 8:5-10.*
a) How often is the Holy Spirit mentioned in these verses?
b) What does He do in relation to the Christian?

DAY 3 *Romans 8:11-17.*
a) Paul enumerates further blessings which belong to those who are 'free' in Christ. What are they?
b) How can we be assured that we are Christians (v.16)?

DAY 4 *Romans 8:18-27.*
a) What are we not free from when we belong to Christ?
b) What makes us endure for Christ's sake (vv.23-25)?
c) When we are weak and ignorant of God's will, who helps us (vv.26-27)?

DAY 5 *Romans 8:28-32.*
a) Do you love and trust the Lord Jesus Christ enough to fully believe verse 28?
b) How would you express God's plan for us as stated in verses 29-30?
c) Do verses 31-32 leave any room for defeat or lack in our lives?

DAY 6 *Romans 8:33-39.*
a) If anyone accuses us, what is our defence?
b) Who is said to love us?
c) Over what things are we assured of victory through Christ?

DAY 7 *John 3:16; 2 Corinthians 5:15,19; Philippians 2:8.*
a) What made God send His Son to die?
b) What did Christ's love for His Father make Him do?
c) What should His love lead us to do?
d) 1 Corinthians 13. Can you see how Christ has freed us from the bondage of self-centredness and started to make us like Him – utterly self-giving?

The great panorama of scriptural freedom spreads out from Deuteronomy 6:23 in ever widening view. God led the people of Israel out from the bondage of Pharaoh and Egypt that they might be led into the land of promise – a land of bountiful provision – a land where they would be free to worship and serve their God.

The portions we have been studying show that God leads us out, too, from the bondage of Satan and the evils of this world and delivers us from our sins and selfishness.

Just as God promised the Israelites 'a land flowing with milk and honey' (Exodus 3:8) so He promises us Heaven (Matthew 7:21). Just as He promised Israel deliverance from their enemies (2 Chronicles 20:17), so He assures us of deliverance from ours. The enemy sin (1 John 1:9), independent self (Romans 7:14-25), the world (Galatians 6:14), the devil (Revelation 12:9-11) have no power over those who are set free in Christ.

God does not promise deliverance from suffering as His witnesses (1 Peter 4:12-19), or as His disciples (2 Corinthians 6:4-6). He also corrects us (Hebrews 12:11). But He does make full provision for us so that we are not overwhelmed (1 Corinthians 10:13) and so we can stand against the evil one and all his thrusts (Ephesians 6:14-18).

As we learn more of His wonderful provision for us (Philippians 4:19) and prove that He will never let us down (Hebrews 13:5) and learn to use His word (Ephesians 6:17) so we trust Him more (Proverbs 3:5) and press on to prove Him more, like Paul (Philippians 3:13-14).

Throughout this study we have seen contrasted human nature under the control of Satan and sin and the same nature turned over to Christ and righteousness. We have seen disobedience against obedience, unbelief against faith, selfishness against self-sacrifice, law against liberty, death against life. We have seen that man at best can only be a slave of sin until the grace of God reaches him and sets him free to obey God.

The chapters in Romans help us glimpse a little of what it means to be captured by Christ and made one with Him. In this relationship of union with Christ (Romans 6) we find real freedom – freedom to serve the living God and real fruitfulness (John 15) – by allowing Christ by His Spirit to be the fruitful One in us. Finally, we find the whole law of God embraced in the law of love – the eternal, self-giving nature of God. In our response to Him, we find the very nature of God being reproduced in us (Galatians 5:13-14).

Michael Green writes in his book *Jesus Spells Freedom*: '... freedom does not mean you can do your own thing, but God's thing, and His thing will involve self-giving for others (for that is His nature). It proves utterly satisfying for the simple reason that it is what we were made for. This is how the best human being who ever lived found His freedom. He lived His life in grateful dependence on the Father who designed and gave it. His service really is perfect freedom, because it is a glad and willing acceptance of our true nature and our ultimate purpose in the world.'

Thy mighty Love, O God, constraineth me,
As some strong tide it presseth on its way.
Seeking a channel in my self-bound soul,
Yearning to sweep all barriers away.

Shall I not yield to that constraining power?
Shall I not say, O tide of Love, flow in?
My God, Thy gentleness hath conquered me,
Life cannot be as it hath hither been.

Break through my nature, mighty, heavenly Love.
Clear every avenue of thought and brain;
Flood my affections, purify my will,
Let nothing but Thine own pure life remain.

Thus wholly mastered and possessed by God,
Forth from my life, spontaneous and free
Shall flow a stream of tenderness and grace,
Loving, because God loves, eternally.

ANSWER GUIDE

The following pages contain an Answer Guide. It is recommended that answers to the questions be attempted before turning to this guide. It is only a guide and the answers given should not be treated as exhaustive.

DAY 1   a) At least four.
                  b) They settled there; Terah died there.

DAY 2   a) Mesopotamia.
                  b) To a 'land' which God would show him.

DAY 3   A great nation, a great name and God's blessing.

DAY 4   a) He moved out in obedience to God.
                  b) Sarai his wife and Lot his nephew are the only two named; the people he
                     had 'acquired' in Haran.
                  c) Seventy-five years old.

DAY 5   a) About 1500 km.
                  b) The land of Canaan.
                  c) The great tree of Moreh.

DAY 6   a) He built an altar to the Lord.
                  b) Personal.

DAY 7   a) By obeying God.
                  b) By disobeying God.

DAY 1   a) They had been reduced to cruel slavery by the Egyptians.
              b) Moses

DAY 2   a) To select a lamb for sacrifice.
              b) It was to be without defect.
              c) The Lord Jesus was sinless.

DAY 3   a) The blood smeared on the lintels and door-posts of their dwellings.
              b) As our Passover lamb.
              c) His blood had to be shed, His life given to redeem us.

DAY 4   a) Personal.
              b) The Angel of Death literally passed over the homes marked with the blood of the lamb.

DAY 5   a) To remind them that God alone had delivered them from their bondage in Egypt.
              b) The death of the Lord Jesus; Jesus is our one sacrifice for sin forever.

DAY 6   a) The Angel of Death struck the Egyptians because they were not protected by the blood of sacrifice – a picture of all who will suffer judgment because they do not trust in Christ's redemptive work.
              b) Pharaoh's willpower is broken and he is so afraid of the power of God that he no longer attempts to oppress the Israelites.

DAY 7   a) They didn't even wait to prepare food for their journey, but borrowed clothes and finance (or its equivalent) from the Egyptians and moved out as fast as possible.
              b) We are to live to please God and not ourselves.

DAY 1   a) No – they were sent out secretly (v.1).
b) No – she even defied and deceived the king's messengers to protect them.
c) Rahab lied outrightly with no scruples, for she was a pagan; Abraham believed God and made his statement in faith that God had a perfect answer.

DAY 2   a) The deliverance at the Red Sea, the defeat of Sihon, the defeat of Og.
b) They were very afraid and began to despair.
Rahab knew the land would fall to the Israelites.

DAY 3   a) Both had a revelation of truth.
b) Yes.
c) The truth. (Personal.)

DAY 4   a) Fear of death; concern for her family circle.
b) Spiritual death which is complete separation from God.
Physical; only God could set her free from her sin.
c) No. They were confident God would give them the land (v.14).

DAY 5   a) To tie the red cord they had used in her window and gather her family together.
b) Yes; specific instructions were to be followed to avoid death.
Through believing in the Lord Jesus Christ.

DAY 6   a) Verse 21: she immediately obeyed their instructions and tied the red cord in the window.
b) Now.
The future is uncertain; we may not live to have another opportunity.
c) Verse 24: they were confident that God had given them the land.

DAY 7   a) Yes.
b) She was to become included as an ancestor of our Lord.
c) Personal.

DAY 1   a) Slaves.
             b) Free them from bondage.
             c) Moses was to bring them out of Egypt.

DAY 2   a) Slavery to Satan.
             We all were at one time slaves as we all have sinned (Romans 3:23).
             Real lasting happiness can only be found in Jesus Christ. Some people
             though appear to be happy with the 'pleasures' that Satan gives them.
             b) We are 'dead' and dead people can do nothing to help themselves.
             Deliverance comes through a divine intervention in our lives.

DAY 3   a) No; basically we are wrong and cut off from God.
             b) The death of Jesus Christ for us; He is our Hope.
             c) The key word is faith; we acknowledge our need and trust in Christ as the
             only One who can free us.

DAY 4   a) They are both slaves.
             b) For the change that had taken place in those to whom he was writing: they
             had been set free from sin.
             c) Personal.

DAY 5   a) Yes (verse 19).
             b) Love – His for us – then ours for Him.
             c) Eternal life instead of death.
             d) Offer themselves wholeheartedly to God.

DAY 6   a) He could be set free.
             b) Love for their master, wife and children made them want to stay.
             An ear was pierced.
             c) A Christian loves God and wants to serve Him for the rest of his or her
             life. This devotion is a deliberate choice and should be visible to all.

DAY 7   a) As turning from idols to serve the living and true God.
             b) Telling others (v.8); waiting for Jesus' return (v.10). It also involved
             suffering (v.6).

DAY 1   a) To dedicate the huge image Nebuchadnezzar had constructed.
                b) Fear of the king's threats; perhaps the influence of the music; everybody else was doing it.

DAY 2   a) They were probably jealous of the positions the king had appointed these three Jews to.
                b) His confidence was in God; He did not retaliate but meekly listened to their accusations.

DAY 3   a) That their God was not able to protect them from his power.
                b) He began to sink and had to cry out for help.

DAY 4   a) Not to serve any 'god' or worship the image of gold.
                It is better to die trusting God than to live denying Him.
                b) They knew they had to speak out the Good News; their intimate knowledge of the Lord and trust in Him was greater than their fear.

DAY 5   a) The king's fury was unleashed on them; they were outnumbered, overpowered, bound and cast helpless into a furnace heated seven times hotter than usual. The odds were all against them.
                b) Rejoice and trust God.

DAY 6   a) The appearance of a fourth person in the fire. There was overwhelming evidence that God was with these men in their situation: they were unbound and unharmed.
                b) To all those who put their trust in God.

DAY 7   a) They had trusted in their God; they had defied the king; and they had been willing to lose their lives rather than fail God.
                b) Nebuchadnezzar was convinced that their God was the true God.

DAY 1   a) After baptism the Holy Spirit had descended on Him, and He had been tempted by the devil in the wilderness.
b) He was a popular teacher in the eyes of the people.

DAY 2   a) He found the particular passage from which He read from.
b) When speaking of the Lord's favour.
He omitted any reference to divine vengeance.
He had come to save and not judge. Divine judgment is reserved to His Second Coming.
c) He said that these Scriptures were being fulfilled before them.

DAY 3   a) Poor, prisoners, blind and oppressed. Bring good news, freedom, sight and release.
b) He was sent by God and was fully anointed by the Holy Spirit.

DAY 4   a) Slavery to sin.
b) Both truth and the Son (Jesus) are mentioned.

DAY 5   a) Spiritual blindess.
It blinds to a true knowledge about Jesus.
b) The Light of the World.

DAY 6   a) They were amazed at Jesus' gracious words.
b) They only recognised Him as Jesus, Joseph's son.

DAY 7   a) They are examples of God blessing people who were not Jews. God had passed His own people by due to their unbelief. The people who were listening to Jesus were unbelievers.
b) They tried to suppress truth and kill Him.
c) Personal. Some people are happy with what they think they know about Jesus but when they let Jesus probe into their heart they can become disturbed by His revelation of their sin and unbelief.

DAY 1 a) Physical death and spiritual death.
b) Spiritual death.
c) Spiritual death (Genesis 3:3 also includes eventual physical death).

DAY 2 a) They were separated from God's presence.
b) Passing from death into life.

DAY 3 a) That it is the end, annihilation.
b) He said there would be a day of judgment after this life.

DAY 4 a) The physical grows old and decays, but the spiritual life of the Christian is renewed and grows stronger.
b) God's presence and love.

DAY 5 a) Because of the joy and the glory that awaited Him.
b) By realising that Jesus suffered too; by focusing on the grace and power He gives us; by remembering that the eternal is more important than the temporary.

DAY 6 a) The fear of death.
b) Through knowing that our relationship with Christ cannot be broken by death, and as He rose again, so will we. The Christian has the Holy Spirit within him.

DAY 7 a) Each of these storms could have resulted in loss of life.
b) The disciples lacked faith and trust and were afraid; Paul believed God's word to him and was able to remain calm.

DAY 1   a) Sin is universal.

b) Lust, abuse of our bodies, perverters of the truth, idolaters, sexual perverts, fornicators, covetousness, self-indulgence, malice, envy, murder, contention, deceit, slander, spite, pride, boasting, disobedience, law-breaking, unloving, delighting in sin.

DAY 2   a) Through the sin of Adam.

b) Adam's act of disobedience makes us sinners.

c) No; by nature we are sinners.

DAY 3   a) The little word 'I'.

b) Sin is self acting independently of God.

DAY 4   a) Those controlled by their 'sinful nature' (actual wording will depend on the translation used).

b) Death.

c) To the devil.

DAY 5   a) He loves us; He died for us (for our sin); He rose again from the dead.

b) Not for themselves but for Jesus Christ. (Notice that this new behaviour did not come about naturally on our part; Christ had to die for us to deal with our sin problem.)

DAY 6   a) As being 'in Christ' and a 'new creation'.

b) Christians should be 'ambassadors' and seek to bring others to the same knowledge of salvation in Christ.

DAY 7   a) Serving Christ, because he knew Jesus Christ as his Saviour.

b) Eternal life and a reward in heaven; we are not lost eternally.

DAY 1   a) It reveals sin in all its ugliness (it is God's standard of holiness). The sentence of death it passes should restrain and deter us from sinning.
b) It shows us our failure to keep God's law. To be released from its condemnation we need to turn to Jesus Christ.

DAY 2   a) We have failed to keep it 100%; we all have sinned.
b) The law condemns, it pronounces a curse: the curse implied here is death.

DAY 3   a) It provokes us to break the law. When told not to do something we are more inclined to do it!
b) No; the law is stated to be holy and the blame lies wholly with us.

DAY 4   a) It cannot justify or make us righteous in God's sight.
b) Having that righteousness that comes from God through faith in Christ.

DAY 5   a) The death of her husband.
b) Our death. This happens when we identify with Christ's death (Romans 6:2-3).

DAY 6   a) Paul says an emphatic no to this suggestion.
b) To serve God in a new way, being enabled to do this by the indwelling of the Holy Spirit?

DAY 7   a) They were abandoning their freedom in Christ to revert back to legalism and keeping the law?
b) They had received the Holy Spirit. He was present among them and they had witnessed miracles accomplished by Him.

DAY 1   a) Those who belong to Christ, that is, those who are 'in' Him'.
b) From the guilt and power of sin and its consequence, death.
c) Sent His own Son in the flesh to die as a sin offering for us.

DAY 2   a) Six times (NIV).
b) He indwells and controls a Christian.

DAY 3   a) The blessings of sonship, access to God's presence in prayer, being led
by the Holy Spirit and future glory. Some see verse 11 as a reference to
healing.
b) The Holy Spirit will give this assurance. Only those who belong to Christ
will have this assurance (v.9).

DAY 4   a) Suffering.
b) The glorious hope of an eternity with Christ and with perfect bodies.
c) The Holy Spirit.

DAY 5   a) Personal.
b) God planned that each one called out of bondage of sin should be
recognised as righteous in Christ and ultimately fully transformed into the
likeness of Christ.
c) No.

DAY 6   a) The truths of God's Word: the death, resurrection and intercession of
Jesus on our behalf is specifically mentioned here.
b) Christ (v.35); God (v.39).
c) Over everything that would separate us from His love.

DAY 7   a) His love for us.
b) Give His life in God's plan of redemption.
c) To live for Him and seek to bring others to Him.
d) Personal.

THE WORD WORLDWIDE

We first heard of WORD WORLDWIDE over 20 years ago when Marie Dinnen, its founder, shared excitedly about the wonderful way ministry to a needy woman had exploded to touch many lives. It was great to see the Word of God being made central in the lives of thousands of men and women, then the life changing effects that resulted when they applied the Word into their circumstances. Over the years the vision for WORD WORLDWIDE has not dimmed in the hearts of those who are involved in this ministry. God is still at work through His Word and in today's self-seeking society, the Word is even more relevant to those who desire true meaning and purpose in life. WORD WORLDWIDE is a ministry of WEC International, an interdenominational missionary society, whose sole purpose for existence is to see Christ known, loved and worshipped by all, particularly those who have yet to hear of His wonderful name. This ministry is a vital part of our work and we warmly recommend the WORD WORLDWIDE 'Geared for Growth' Bible studies to you. We know that as you study His Word you will be enriched in your personal walk with Christ. It is our hope that as you are blessed through these studies, you will find opportunities to help others find a personal relationship with Jesus. As a mission we would encourage you to work with us to make Christ known to the ends of the earth.

Stewart & Jean Moulds – British Directors, WEC International.

A full list of over 50 'Geared for Growth' studies can be obtained from:

ENGLAND　　John & Ann Edwards
　　　　　　　5 Louvain Terrace, Hetton-le Hole, Tyne & Wear, DH5 9PP
　　　　　　　Tel. 0191 5262803　　Email: rhysjohn.edwards@virgin.net

IRELAND　　Steffney Preston
　　　　　　　33 Harcourts Hill, Portadown, Craigavon, N. Ireland, BT62 3RE
　　　　　　　Tel. 028 3833 7844　　Email: sa.preston@talk21.com

SCOTLAND　　Margaret Halliday
　　　　　　　10 Douglas Drive, Newton Mearns, Glasgow, G77 6HR
　　　　　　　Tel. 0141 639 8695　　Email: m_halliday@excite.co.uk

WALES　　William & Eirian Edwards
　　　　　　　Penlan Uchaf, Carmarthen Road, Kidwelly, Carms., SA17 5AF
　　　　　　　Tel. 01554 890423　　Email: Penlan.uchaf@farming.co.uk

UK CO-ORDINATOR
Anne Jenkins, 2 Windermere Road, Carnforth, Lancs., LA5 9AR
Tel. 01524 734797　　Email: anne@jenkins.abelgratis.com

www.wordworldwide.org.uk